Amelia Bloomer

A Photo-Illustrated Biography
by Mary J. Lickteig

Content Consultant:
Andrea Libresco
Department of Curriculum and Teaching
Hofstra University

Bridgestone Books
an imprint of Capstone Press

Fast Facts about Amelia Bloomer

- Amelia Bloomer spoke and wrote against the use of alcohol. Alcohol is a strong chemical found in certain drinks.
- Amelia was a leader in the fight for women's rights.
- Bloomers is another name for a style of baggy pants. Bloomers are named after Amelia.

Bridgestone Books are published by Capstone Press
818 North Willow Street, Mankato, Minnesota 56001
http://www.capstone-press.com
Copyright ©1998 by Capstone Press. All rights reserved.
No part of this book may be reproduced without written permission from the publisher.
The publisher takes no responsibility for the use of any of the materials
or methods described in this book, nor for the products thereof.
Printed in the United States of America.

Library of Congress Cataloging-in-Publication Data
Lickteig, Mary J.
    Amelia Jenks Bloomer : a photo-illustrated biography / by Mary J. Lickteig.
        p. cm. -- (Read and discover photo-illustrated biographies)
    Includes bibliographical references and index.
    Summary: A biography of the temperance leader and women's rights advocate who spent her
life trying to improve social conditions for women.
    ISBN 1-56065-747-2
    1. Bloomer, Amelia Jenks, 1818-1894. 2. Feminists--United States--Biography--
Juvenile literature. 3. Women's rights--United States--History--Juvenile literature.
4. Temperance--United States--History--Juvenile literature. [1. Bloomer, Amelia Jenks, 1818-1894.
2. Feminists. 3. Women--Biography. 4. Women's rights.]
I. Title II. Series
HQ1413.B6L53   1998
305.42'092--dc21
[B]   97-41512
                                                                                  CIP
                                                                                   AC

Editorial Credits: Editor, Greg Linder; cover design, Timothy Halldin; photo research, Michelle L.
Norstad
Photo credits: Archive Photos, cover, 4, 14 (inset); Corbis-Bettmann, 10, 12; Council Bluffs Public
Library, 16; Seneca Falls Historical Society, 6, 8, 14, 18; Sophia Smith Collection, Smith College, 20

Table of Contents

A Woman for Women's Rights

Amelia Bloomer worked to improve the lives of women. Amelia lived at a time when women could not vote. They could not hold government offices or own property. Most colleges would not accept women as students. A college is a school people go to after high school. Most women were expected to stay home instead of getting jobs.

Amelia believed women should have the same rights as men. She gave speeches and wrote articles about her beliefs. She started the first newspaper for women.

Amelia tried to help people in another way. She worked in the Temperance Movement. A movement is a group of people that supports a cause. People in the Temperance Movement were against the use of alcohol. Alcohol is a strong chemical found in certain drinks.

Amelia Bloomer started the first newspaper for women.

Early Years

Amelia Jenks was born May 27, 1818, in Homer, New York. Her father Ananias Jenks worked in a clothing store. Amelia had three sisters and two brothers.

Amelia went to school for only a few years. She learned to read and write. Amelia's mother Lucy taught her other things. She taught Amelia to be honest and kind. She taught Amelia that all people should have the same rights.

Amelia became a teacher at the age of 17. After a year, she moved to Waterloo, New York. There, she took care of children in other people's homes. She made many friends. One of them was a young man named Dexter Bloomer. In 1840, she married Dexter. Amelia Jenks became Amelia Bloomer.

After the wedding, Amelia and Dexter moved to Seneca Falls, New York. Dexter wrote for a newspaper there.

Amelia married Dexter Bloomer in 1840.

On this spot stood the Wesleyan Chapel where the First Woman's Rights Convention in the World's history was held July 19 and 20 1848.

Elizabeth Cady Stanton moved this resolution which was seconded by Frederick Douglass: "That it is the duty of the women of this country to secure to themselves their sacred right to the elective franchise"

A Meeting in Seneca Falls

In 1840, Dexter worked to help William Henry Harrison become president. Amelia helped Dexter. She wrote slogans and made signs.

Dexter asked Amelia to write articles for the Seneca Falls newspaper. She did not think she could do it. Dexter told her to try. Soon Amelia was writing articles for many newspapers.

Amelia attended the first women's rights convention in 1848. A convention is a meeting for people with the same interests. About 300 men and women attended this convention in Seneca Falls.

The people at the convention wrote an important paper. It was called the Declaration of Sentiments. The paper said that men and women should be treated equally. It said that colleges should accept women as students. The paper also said that women should vote and have jobs.

Amelia attended the first women's rights convention in 1848.

The Lily

Amelia helped start the Ladies Temperance Society in 1848. Members of this group did not want people to drink alcohol. They believed that drinking alcohol was bad for people's health. They felt that men who drank treated women and children badly.

At the first meeting, the women decided to start a newspaper. All of the women said they would help. They called their newspaper *The Lily*.

Producing the newspaper was hard work. Most of the women quit. Only one woman helped Amelia. She helped the first time *The Lily* was printed. Then she quit, too.

Amelia worked on *The Lily* for more than five years. She found other women to help. It was the first newspaper written for women. It was also the first newspaper written by women. At first, it featured articles about people who opposed drinking. Later, many articles talked about women's rights.

Members of the Ladies Temperance Society felt that men who drank alcohol treated women badly.

Writer and Speech Maker

In 1849, Dexter became the postmaster in Seneca Falls. A postmaster is a person in charge of a post office. Dexter hired Amelia to be his assistant. At the time, women did not have jobs like this. But Dexter knew Amelia could do it.

Amelia worked in the post office for four years. She kept producing *The Lily*. Amelia made sure the newspaper was printed and mailed. She wrote articles about education and woman suffrage. Suffrage is the right to vote.

Other women started writing for *The Lily*. Elizabeth Cady Stanton and Susan B. Anthony wrote articles. They were two leaders of woman suffrage.

Amelia made speeches about women's rights. She spoke in New York City, Chicago, and many other cities. In some places, people were shocked. They had never seen a woman give a speech before.

Amelia made speeches about women's rights.

Bloomers

In the 1850s, people expected women to wear long skirts. The skirts dragged on the ground. Women had to be careful or they would trip and fall.

In 1851, Elizabeth Cady Stanton's cousin visited Seneca Falls. Her name was Libby Miller. Libby wore a short dress with long, baggy pants underneath. Amelia saw Libby in her outfit at the post office.

Amelia wrote an article for *The Lily*. She told readers how to make the new outfit. She printed a drawing of the dress and pants. She wrote that more women should wear these outfits. Amelia herself wore the outfits for the next eight years.

Other newspapers printed stories about the new clothing style. Writers named the pants bloomers after Amelia Bloomer.

Many men did not think women should wear pants. Some of these men threw eggs or stones at women who wore bloomers.

Writers named bloomers after Amelia.

The Western Home Visitor

Amelia and Dexter lived in Seneca Falls for 14 years. They moved when Dexter bought a newspaper in Mount Vernon, Ohio. The newspaper's name was *The Western Home Visitor*. Amelia helped Dexter produce the newspaper. She also kept working on *The Lily*.

The Bloomers printed both newspapers on a large printing press. A printing press is a machine that makes copies. The Bloomers needed more workers to run the press. They hired a new worker named Mrs. C. W. Lundy.

The men who ran the printing press quit their jobs. They refused to work with a woman. They wanted the Bloomers to fire Mrs. Lundy. For a time, both newspapers shut down.

Amelia and Dexter did not do what the men wanted. Instead, they hired three more women and three new men. Mrs. Lundy kept her job. It was another way the Bloomers helped women gain rights.

Amelia helped Dexter produce *The Western Home Visitor*. They hired women to print it.

A Move to Iowa

In 1855, the Bloomers moved west to Council Bluffs, Iowa. They wanted to live in a new place. At that time, not many settlers lived in Iowa. It had large areas of unsettled land.

Dexter and Amelia took a train from Ohio to Illinois. The railroad did not go any farther. The Bloomers crossed the Mississippi River on a steamboat. They landed in St. Louis, Missouri.

The Bloomers wanted to continue by boat. They got as far as St. Joseph, Missouri. The river was too low to go any farther. Next, they took a stagecoach from St. Joseph to Council Bluffs. The trip from Ohio to Council Bluffs took 26 days.

Amelia shared her ideas along the way. The Bloomers stopped in many towns. People in these towns wanted Amelia to give speeches. She spoke again and again about temperance and women's rights.

The Bloomers moved to Iowa in 1855.

A Better Life for Women

The Bloomers spent the rest of their lives in Council Bluffs. Amelia made bandages and clothing for soldiers during the Civil War (1861-1865). In 1870, Iowa women chose Amelia to be a leader. They elected her vice president of the Iowa National Woman Suffrage Association. This group worked to gain voting rights for women.

Amelia Bloomer died on December 30, 1894. Women still did not have the right to vote. But life was better for women. Women could attend more colleges. Women could have jobs. Women could own property in some states.

The U.S. Congress makes laws for the whole country. In 1920, Congress passed the 19th Amendment to the Constitution of the United States. This law gave women the right to vote. Many women had worked hard to gain this important right. Amelia Bloomer was one of those women.

Amelia Bloomer helped women gain the right to vote.

Words from Amelia Bloomer

"It is right for any American woman to occupy the Presidential Chair at Washington."
From *The Lily*.

"Our counsel to every woman is, wear what pleases you best."
From *The Lily*.

"While [woman] demands a law that entirely prohibits traffic in strong drink, let her also obtain a right to a voice in making all laws by which she is to be governed."
From *The Lily*

"[God] has created woman intelligent and responsible and given her a great work to do, and woe unto her if she does not!"
From a speech given in Metropolitan Hall, New York, 1853.

Important Dates in Amelia Bloomer's Life

1818—Born on May 27 in Homer, New York

1840—Marries Dexter Bloomer

1848—Attends the first women's rights convention in Seneca Falls

1849—Starts a newspaper called *The Lily*

1849—Begins working in the Seneca Falls post office

1851—Advises women to wear bloomers

1852—Delivers her first public speech in Rochester, New York

1853—Delivers a temperance speech at Metropolitan Hall in New York

1854—Moves to Mount Vernon, Ohio

1855—Moves to Council Bluffs, Iowa

1870—Elected vice president of the Woman Suffrage Association of Iowa

1894—Dies in Council Bluffs, Iowa

Words to Know

alcohol (AL-kuh-hol)—a strong chemical found in certain drinks

bloomers (BLOOM-urs)—long, baggy pants worn by women

Congress (KONG-griss)—the part of the U.S. government that makes laws for the entire country

convention (kuhn-VEN-shuhn)—a meeting for people with the same interests

movement (MOOV-muhnt)—a group of people that supports a cause

postmaster (POHST-mas-tur)—a person in charge of a post office

printing press (PRIN-ting PRES)—a machine used to make copies

suffrage (SUFF-ruhj)—the right to vote

Read More

Blumberg, Rhoda. *Bloomers!* New York: Bradbury Press, 1993.

Johnston, Norma. *Remember the Ladies: The First Women's Rights Convention.* New York: Scholastic, 1995.

McCully, Emily Arnold. *The Ballot Box Battle.* New York: Alfred A. Knopf, 1996.

St. George, Judith. *By George, Bloomers!* Crozet, Va.: Shoe Tree Press, 1989.

Useful Addresses and Internet Sites

Women's Rights National Historical Park
136 Fall Street
Seneca Falls, NY 13148

National Women's Hall of Fame
76 Fall Street
Seneca Falls, NY 13148

Amelia Bloomer
http://www.nps.gov/wori/bloomer.htm

Encyclopedia of Women's History
http://www.teleport.com/~megaines/women.html

Woman's Suffrage
http://www.historychannel.com/community/woman/

Index